100 CONVERSATION STARTERS

PRACTICAL HELP FOR SHARING YOUR FAITH

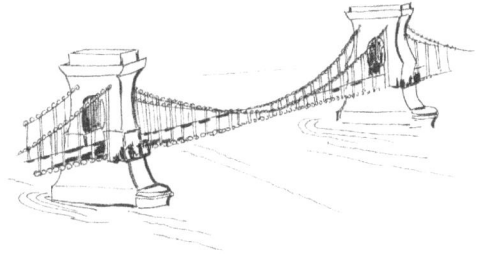

RORY KAYE & PETER STRAND

100 Conversation Starters
Practical Help for Sharing Your Faith
by Rory Kaye and Peter Strand

Signalman Publishing
www.signalmanpublishing.com
email: info@signalmanpublishing.com
Kissimmee, Florida

© Rory Kaye & Peter Strand 2012
All rights reserved.

Foreword and prayers by: Rory Kaye

Designed by: Dynamic Art© (www.dynamicart.se)

Illustrations by Helena Backmark, Maria Gunnarsson & Alexandra Ciriák

Co-workers: Martin Gunnarsson & Maria Gunnarsson

ISBN: 978-1-935991-47-2 (paperback)
        978-1-935991-48-9 (ebook)

Printed in the United States of America

Thank you God for creating us. Thank you Yeshua (Jesus) for becoming one of us and enduring the cross, so that we could become part of your family forever. Thank you for giving us your Spirit so we can know you and get help to do your will.

Thanks to my beautiful wife, Gunilla, and our children: Elana, David & his wife Sara, Sarah Michelle, Ariel, Jasmine and Raphael Aaron, for all of your love; and to Peter for making this book happen.

—Rory Kaye

Thanks to Hit Gyülekezete, a big and loving church where God's presence wonderfully dwells in Budapest, Hungary. Thank you for inspiration to complete this book for the last days' soulwinners.

—Peter Strand

Table of Contents

Forward

Conversation Starters 8

Praying for People 110

Praying with People...111

Recommended Books..112

Recommended Websites..114

Help us to become better 115

Foreword

Jesus said to His disciples that if they loved Him, they'd obey Him. "Love one another, preach the gospel" and teach their disciples to do the same. Yet, in a 2011 survey, a third of all believers asked, had never once shared the gospel, or even their testimony, with a non-believer. Practical help is needed. That's why this book was written.

Most of us have experienced the frustration of not knowing what to say or how to get started. But we can learn to start conversations by using associations from everyday life; to share our faith in a way that is easy for others to understand. Jesus did this. He invited fishermen to become fishers of men. To a woman drawing water from a well, He offered living water that would never run dry. With the help of the Holy Spirit, Jesus knew just what to say and how to relate to every person He met.

The same Spirit that enabled Jesus to hear and perceive what His Father wanted said and done, is now inside of each of His disciples! Disciples believe they are forgiven by faith in what Jesus did on the cross. We grow into maturity as we become increasingly reliant on God's Spirit to help us do our Father's will instead of our own.

The Holy Spirit is our Rabbi (teacher), our helper and comforter. His desire is to fill us with God's love, peace, joy, wisdom and power. That power is the boldness we need to speak and act in accordance with the Father's will. "For as many as are led by the Spirit of God, these are sons of God... being conformed to the image of His Son." Our responsibility is to ask God for wisdom and not doubt His unchanging generosity. The Spirit will help us "build bridges" for people, that make the kingdom of God more understandable so that, when they're ready, they can "cross over" to become His children.

If we follow the Holy Spirit's leading, God will connect us to people in a multitude of ways; through: friendship, humor, kindness, compassion; words of knowledge and wisdom; prayers for them and with them for their salvation, healing, deliverance and even miracles. The goodness of God leads people to repentance. He prepares the "soil" of their hearts to receive the "good seed" of the gospel. How well that seed takes root is dependent upon the quality of the soil and the discipling or "watering" in the Word that occurs after sowing.

Jesus is the same, yesterday, today and forever. He still forgives, heals, delivers and baptizes in the Holy Spirit. The Comforter helps us become secure in the Father's love, no matter how much we fail; then to grow in grace unto maturity. We're called to be transformed through the renewing of our minds, into receivers of God's love and revelation, and then freely give to others of the overflow of His presence in our lives. Jesus baptizes us with holy fire as well, making us holy, and fervent in spirit, love, prayer and evangelism.

We're not alone in any of this either. God has appointed angels to help each of us who are inheriting salvation. Every one of us have divinely prepared assignments and appointments waiting to be kept. We therefore encourage you to pray **for** people while you're speaking with them, if they're open for you to do so. God has been waiting for them. Your prayers and His answers will help them to experience His love and presence; even prepare them to be saved. If they're ready, be bold to pray together **with** them to give their lives to the Lord as well. If they do so, all the angels in heaven will rejoice!

Not everyone will want to talk, believe your message or be open to receiving prayer. Sometimes you'll be mocked. In some countries, these conversations could even get you arrested, but God will give you more of His heart for the lost as you begin to talk to people.

You will not always have time for a whole conversation, but even just seven words, shared in His love, can bear eternal fruit:

"May God bless you; He loves you!"

Rory Kaye, Gothenburg, Sweden

Abortion
Abort Every Sin

(Your acquaintance is asking if believers are against abortion)
Actually, some abortions are necessary. Never aborting babies, but every evil plan and action in our lives! We must abort them all or else Heaven will be closed for us.

What do you mean?
Evil plans, bitterness and unforgiven sin are the most dangerous things that anyone can have in their life, because they stop us from knowing God and going to Heaven. The good news is that it's possible to be free and forgiven.

How can that happen?
It begins by forgiveness. Only God can forgive sins, and He sent Jesus to die on the cross to fully pay the penalty for all our sins. When we believe in Him, we can receive God's Spirit, who gives us the power to turn away from every evil thought and action.

Hmm...
When Jesus died, He took upon Himself all our sin; all the things we've done that separate us from other people and our Creator.

I understand.
What God wants us to do is to receive forgiveness and turn away from sin. From the moment we are forgiven, we can stand guiltless before our Creator and are then able to receive His Spirit into our lives, who enables us to know and to do God*s will. Do you want to abort the sin in your heart today?

Absolutely.
May I help you talk to God right now?
Please do.

Adoption
God wants to adopt you

(Your friend is talking about someone who has adopted a baby)
Have I told you that I'm also adopted?
What do you mean?
I'm adopted by my Heavenly Father!
Adopted by your Heavenly Father?
Yes, He has a family; all who have given their lives to Him through faith in Jesus.
Hmm...
The bad news is that we're separated from Him by our sin. The good news is that we are welcome; He wants us to come to Him. He wants to 'adopt' us into His family! The way we come to Him is through His Son Jesus.
Go on...
He was sent from Heaven to Earth to be crucified and die. When Jesus died, He took upon Himself all the things that we've done that separate us from our Creator. What you need to do is to turn away from all that is evil, turn to God and put your trust in what Jesus did for you on the cross. From that moment, you will be "born again" into God's family and on your way to Heaven!
I've never heard before that God has a family!
He does, and He wants you to be a part of it. Do you want to be?
Absolutely.
May I help you talk to God right now?
Yes, please.

Alarm tag
The alarm will sound!

Have you ever been in a store when someone tries to leave with an alarm tag still attached to their clothing?
Yes, I've seen that, and heard it too!
It's a good picture of how it will be when someone tries to enter
Heaven while still living in their sin. The alarm will sound!
Do you really think so?
Yes, although it won't sound like it does in the store. The Bible says that everyone has sinned, and that no one living in sin can enter into Heaven. During an average lifespan, even if we only sinned once a day, we would have more than 25,000 sins with us when we stand before God.
Hmm...
Can you understand that the alarm will be sounding, so to speak?
Yes, but what can I do about it?
God wants you to believe that He sent Jesus to die on the cross, to set you free from your sins. Turn to Him and put your trust in God. Then you will be forgiven and welcomed into Heaven.
I understand.
Do you want to be forgiven and come to Heaven?
Absolutely!
The same Holy Spirit that was in Jesus wants to come into you as well. He'll help you: to know God's will for your life, and to become the man/woman He created you to be! May I help you talk to God right now?
I'd like that, thanks.

Architect
Every creation needs a Creator

This is a really beautiful building!
You're right. You know, every building has it's architect.
That's true.
… and every painting, it's painter.
Yes.
… and all of creation has it's Creator!
I get your point.
The bad news is that man is separated from his Creator, because of sin in our lives.
And the good news?
The Creator became one of us, lived a perfect life, and died on a cross, to cancel all the things we've done that separate us from Him. Jesus did this so that we can be forgiven and rightly related with God!
How?
By believing in His sacrifice on the cross, and by welcoming Him
into our lives as Lord. Do you want to do that?
Yes.
God wants to fill you with His Spirit as well, so that you can know His will and fulfill your destiny on earth! May I help you talk to Him right now?
You mean pray, right? Okay, but you pray please.

Bag
The heaviest burden

(Noticing someone carrying a heavy bag)
Is your bag heavy?
You're not kidding!
Do you know the heaviest burden anyone's ever carried?
No idea...
It was when Jesus carried all the sins of the world on the cross.
I don't understand.
He did it for a reason; so that we could get rid of everything that stops us from going to Heaven. Heaven is a holy place and no one living in sin can enter there, but the good news is that we can call upon Jesus for forgiveness and salvation and enter in.
Really?
God doesn't want us to live in our sins and absolutely not to die in them, but wants to carry them away from us. Do you know how?
Please tell me.
First we need to make a decision to turn away from what we know is wrong and then call upon Jesus for forgiveness and salvation. Do you want to do that?
Absolutely.
God will never leave you. He wants to also fill you with His Spirit and live on the inside of you. The Spirit of God will give you the help you need in this life. May I help you talk to God right now?
Yes, please.

Bananas
It's what's inside that counts

(Having a banana)
Do you know what's similar between people and bananas?
What do you mean?
It's what's on the inside that counts and inside us is the most important part, our spirit.
Why is that most important?
Because it is eternal and it'll go somewhere when life here is over.
Where will it go then?
To God or away from God and that depends on one thing only.
If you are a good person?
Many think so, but that is not the case. Man's goodness is not good enough to get Him into Heaven. The good news is that there is a Savior, the Lord Jesus Christ. If He is Lord of our lives, we can come to Heaven.
What do you mean by 'Lord'?
I trust Him that He knows better than us what's right in every area of life. With His help, I am able to do what He wants me to do.
I think I understand.
God wants you to turn to Him and believe in what Jesus did on the cross. He was God's sacrifice to provide forgiveness for all the sins of the world; even yours. From that moment, you will be on your way to Heaven.
Hmm...
Do you want to belong to God and come to Heaven?
Definitely.
Shall we talk to God right now, you and I?
Sure.

Bathroom
Makes our hearts clean

(Someone has just been to the bathroom)
Have you ever been in a bathroom where the toilet didn't work?
Yes, frustrating!
It is; but it's also a picture of how frustrating it is to try to cleanse
our own hearts clean without God's help to remove unforgiven sin.
Hmm...
Sin is not only rape and murder, but also impure thoughts, evil
words, lies, hate, pride, greed, jealousy, bitterness, selfishness,etc.
I see.
The good news is that God wants to make our hearts clean. This is possible because of what Jesus did for us on the cross, when He took all the sins of mankind upon Himself.
Yes, I believe that.
Great, but if you want to have your heart cleansed, you need to turn to God, ask forgiveness for your sins and make Jesus Lord of your life. This is how you can receive forgiveness and have your heart cleansed. You can also receive God's Spirit and go to Heaven. Do you want all this?
Yes, absolutely.
May I help you talk to God right now?
Please do.

Blind
Blind to the truth

(A *blind man walks past*)
Did you know that I was once blind?
Really?
Not physically, but blind to the most important truth of all. I thought
I was good enough to go to Heaven as I was.
But you are a good person...
Comparing with some people, yes, but comparing with God's standard for good, good enough for Heaven, not even close... Heaven is God's house, it is a perfect place and only if we are perfect in His eyes we can come in there!
Who can come in then?
No one, by his own goodness, but there is another way; the way of forgiveness. This forgiveness was made possible for us when Jesus offered Himself on the cross!
Hmm...
When we believe in that and turn away from what is not pleasing to
God, we are forgiven and on the way to Heaven!
I understand.
May I help you talk to God right now?
I'd appreciate that.

Body part
Your most important part

(Talking to a sportsman)
You have a strong body, but do you know the part of you which is most important?
The heart, or perhaps the brain?
They are indeed important, but the most important part of us is our spirit, the part of us that lives forever!
I'm not sure that we have a spirit.
Well, people have different opinions about this, but the Word of God says that our body is a kind of house where we live during our time on earth. When life here is over, man's spirit leaves the body.
Leaves where, to Heaven?
That's God's will for everyone and the good news is that it's possible for everyone to go to Heaven; the choice is yours.
What do you mean?
Jesus said that He is the only way to Heaven. He is the way, because He is the only one who can forgive us from our sins.
Hmm...
The moment you ask Jesus to be the Lord and Savior of your life, you belong to God and your spirit will leave for Heaven when your days here are over.
I understand.
One part of God is His Holy Spirit. He will come into your life to strengthen you and help you to live your life with God and fulfill the destiny He has for you. Do you want to experience this?
I do.
May I help you to talk with God right now?
Please do that.

Book
The core message

(Somebody is reading a book)
Do you know which book is the most read throughout history, even today; with more than one billion copies in print?
The Bible?
That's right, but did you know that even if it's over 1,000 pages long, the core message is just two things.
What's that?
After creating the world, God became separated from man because of sin in the heart of man, but He bridged the gap by sending Jesus to die on the cross.
I really appreciate your explanation. I have never heard it like this before.
Thank you. This became personal for me some years ago. You also need to make it personal for you.
Whether you believe it or not, one day we will all stand before God; the only way to come into Heaven is to make Jesus Lord of your life.
So you mean I don't belong to God yet?
Not yet; that only happens by an act of your own will. We are all created in His image, but it's our choice if we want to become part of His family.
Hmm...
Please don't miss God's plan for you.
How do I get started? May I pray with you? Sure.

Brainwashed
He washed my heart clean

(Somebody confronts you about your faith)
I heard that you have become a Jesus freak, have they brainwashed you totaly?
Haha, no, I am not brainwashed, but my heart have been washed clean, the things that I had open my heart and life for that made me dirty before God have been forgiven!
So in your eyes, I am a big sinner?
My friend, we are all in need of forgivness. I am not better then you in any way. The difference is that I have said 'yes' to the forgivness that God offers us.
Hmm....
This forgivness became possible because of what Jesus did on the cross. God sent Him for a reason, the reason was to die for all the sins of the world, for yours and for mine!
I understand
God is not looking for perfect people, He is looking for people that is humble, humble enough to admit that they have sinned against Him and that they need forgivness. When He finds these people he becomes so happy, He gives they forgivness and washes their hearts totaly clean from all sin, guilt and darkness!
I wish I could believe...
It is easy to believe, let us ask God to give you that faith.
Okay.

Bridge
God has built a bridge

(Seeing a bridge)
Did you know that just as different parts of a city can be separated from each other, God and man are separated too.
Are we? I thought God loved everyone?
He does, but just as water separates different parts of some cities, God and man are separated by sin in the heart of man: impure thoughts, evil words, lies, gossip, hate, pride, greed, bitterness, jealousy, selfishness, etc.
But I haven't sinned so much.
The problem is that any unforgiven sin separates us from God. The good news is that He has also built a bridge! That bridge is Jesus and because of what He did for us on the cross, there is now a bridge to God.
I'm happy for you that you have found that bridge, I don't believe in this...
I can only speak from personal experience. When I turned to Jesus something very real happened to me. He came into my life, took away my guilt and shame and began to change my life. I felt like coming home!
It sounds fantastic, what did you do?
I decided to turn away from what I knew was not pleasing to God and put my trust in what Jesus did for me on the cross.
Perhaps I can experience this also?
Absolutely, God sees that your heart is open and that you want the truth. Can I pray for you?
Yes please.

Broken
The relationship is broken

(Something is broken)
Hmm, it's broken...
It's never fun when things break, but do you know what would be the worst thing to break?
No, please tell me.
It's when we break the relationship with our Creator. We break it with sin, such as hate, lies, lust, pride, greed, jealousy, selfishness, unforgiveness, stealing etc.
Hmm...
The bad news is that we have all broken the relationship with our Creator. The good news is that He did something so that the relationship could be healed again! Do you know what He did?
No...
He sent Jesus to live a perfect life and then die and to take upon Himself all the things we have done that broke the relationship.
I understand.
What we must do is to turn away from those things and put our trust in what Jesus did for us on the cross. From that moment the relationship becomes repaired. Do you want your relationship with God healed today?
Absolutely.
May I help you talk to God right now?
Please do.

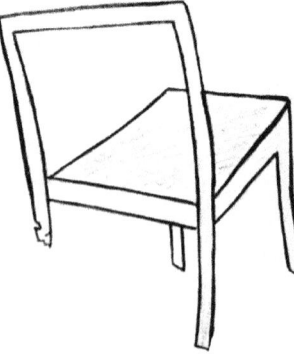

Bus driver
Created for fellowship with God

(They are telling a joke)
Have you heard the joke about the priest and the bus driver?
No, please tell me.
A priest and a bus-driver both went to Heaven. The priest was very upset to find himself on the 15th row while the bus-driver was on the first, so he said to God 'I have talked about you all my life. How come I am on the 15th row and the bus-driver is on the first?'
'Well' God said, 'when you preached, everybody fell asleep but when he drove, everyone was praying!'
That's funny!
Yes, but there is also an important truth in it. Man is created for fellowship with God. Prayer is talking to God. Our fellowship with God begins when we turn to Him in prayer and put our trust in Jesus.
Does it?
Yes, many people think that it's good deeds that will connect us with God, but the Bible says that we must come to Him through faith.
I understand.
God wants you to begin your relationship with Him today. Do you know how?
Not exactly.
When Jesus died on the cross He took upon Himself all the things that separate Him and man. What we need to do is to believe that He did this for us.
Okay.
Shall we talk to God together now?
Sure.

Butterfly
A fascinating creation

(Seeing a butterfly)
I love butterflies; they are like flying works of art!
You're right.
The creation is really fascinating: dotted dogs, striped horses, the dragonfly like a little helicopter and of course the handsome penguin in tuxedo!
Haha, I totally agree!
There was a reason God created this world and it was because He wanted fellowship with man.
I believe in God, I pray every day.
Do you read your Bible?
Sorry to say, it was many years ago...
Do you live in holiness?
Not all the time...
Friend, the Bible says that without holiness no one will see the Lord. Jesus also said: 'Not everyone who says to me "Lord, Lord" will enter the Kingdom of Heaven, but only, he who does the will of my Father who is in Heaven.'
Hmm...
We need to do something more than believe, we also need to repent. Turn 180 degrees away from sin to God and trust in Jesus. Then God will give us both forgiveness and the gift of His Spirit. He will help us to know and do God's will. Do you want to give your life to Him today?
Yes, I want to do that.
May I pray together with you?
Please do.

Che Guevara
The ultimate freedom fighter

(Someone is wearing a Che Guevara button)
I see that you admire freedom fighters.
Yes, I believe freedom is the most important thing in life. Absolutely, but do you know who is the ultimate freedom fighter? Nelson Mandela perhaps, or Martin Luther King?
They were indeed great, but there is one greater. His name is Jesus. God sent Him to this world to set all mankind free from the chains of sin. On the cross He made it possible for us to be free from sin, have a good conscience before God and go to Heaven! **Hmm...**
He wants you to live in freedom on this Earth, but He also wants to set you totally free from being oppressed by sin, and forgive you the things that now separate you from Him!
I understand.
Do you want to experience this freedom that God has for you?
Absolutely.
What God wants you to do is to turn away from what the Word of God says is wrong, and turn to the Savior, turn to Jesus. May I help you talk to God right now?
Please.

Chimney
Get the poison out

(Seeing a chimney)
Do you know why houses have chimneys?
To get the smoke and poison out of course.
Yes, and we are like houses; we have opened our hearts and lives for 'poison'; for things not pleasing to God. If we do not get them out, it will stop us from going to Heaven!
Hmm...
But just like the chimney makes it possible for a house to get the poison out; God made it possible for us to get the 'poison' and sin out of our lives. Do you know how?
Not really...
By sending Jesus to die for all the sins of man! We need to say goodbye to sin and welcome the Savior Jesus Christ into our lives! From that day we are forgiven and on the way to Heaven!
Sounds good!
God's own Spirit will be your Helper to live a life that makes God happy and to fulfill your destiny here on earth. May I help you talk to Him right now?
Please do.

Clover
He had to come down

(Looking at a clover patch)
Did you know that the three leaf clover is the symbol of Ireland?
No, I have never heard that.
A man named Patrick, a missionary from England, explained the
Trinity for the Irish people using clover.
I see.
Do you know why God had to reveal Himself in three persons: Father, Son and Holy Spirit?
No idea.
Jesus came down to us to die for the sins of the world. His death on the cross provides forgiveness for all the things we've done that separate us from His Father. When we believe in Jesus, God
gives us His Spirit as well, who helps us to know and to do His will. Jesus died for us all, you know; for you and for me.
Yes, I have heard that many times.
Just hearing it will not help you. Forgiveness for sin, forgiveness for breaking God's law and escaping to be condemned is only offered by turning away from what we know is wrong and by putting our trust in Jesus.
Perhaps I will do it when I'm older...
It's not sure that you will be older, we don't have tomorrow for sure, then it might be too late and you'd miss Heaven.
You sound serious.
We're talking about Heaven and Hell, my friend.
What shall I do then?
Be honest with God. May I help you talk to Him right now?
Sure.

Coffee
Wakes you up

(Drinking coffee)
Do you know the similarity between coffee and the Bible?
No idea...
They both wake you up!
Hmm...
Some people drink coffee in the morning to wake themselves up. A
passage from the Bible woke me up some years ago.
What do you mean?
When Jesus says, that He is the only way to the Father. It's not by trying to be good enough that we will come to Heaven. It is only
by Jesus; by turning to Him and believing in what He did on the cross when He died for our sins, for all the things we had done that separate us from God.
Interesting.
Are you awake to this truth, that you need to turn to Jesus and trust Him instead of trusting your own goodness, in order to go to Heaven?
I guess I am now.
May I help you talk to God right now?
Sure thing.

Crime
We are all guilty

(Somebody is mentioning a criminal act)
Do you know that we are all guilty?
What do you mean?
We are all guilty, because we have broken God's law.
God's law?
Yes, the ten commandments. We break them with impure thoughts,
evil words and lies, pride, hate, selfishness, greed, jealousy etc.
We are all, more or less guilty.
But God is love, He will forgive everyone.
Well, the truth is that forgiveness is possible for everyone, but it is not automatic. We have an important part in it. Our part is to turn away from what is not pleasing to God and welcome Jesus into our lives.
I don't think God will condemn anyone.
God wants everyone to go to Heaven, but people living in sin can never enter the place where God lives. The good news is that He sent Jesus to be crucified and die, so that we through Him can get forgiveness and enter Heaven.
You mean it's only to call upon Him?
He is so close to everyone, when you open your mouth to speak to
Him you can be sure that He hears you. Shall we do that now?
Yes.

Cross
Requirement for Heaven

(Somebody is wearing a cross around their neck)
You have a nice cross; are you a believer?
Yes, I am.
Can I ask you something, what must I do to go to Heaven?
I would say to have a good heart.
It's great to have a good heart, the problem is the bad things we have done, because they can't enter Heaven together with us. **Hmm…**
Therefore it is not enough to be good, we need someone who takes away the bad things we have done. That was the reason Jesus came and offered Himself on the cross. He paid the price for sin and because He did that, He is now able to forgive sin.
Hmm…
So it's not about our goodness, it's about His goodness. It's not about what we can do, but what He has done.
I understand, you make it very clear.
Let us pray together, and ask Jesus to be the Lord of your life, and for God's Spirit to help you know and do God's perfect will.
Sure.

Death
What happens after death?

(Speaking about someone that has died)
How old was he/she?
80.
Did you know that the oldest people in the world today live to be around 120 years old?
Yes, I have read that.
Do you know why?
No idea?
God made it that way. It says so in the first book in the Bible, called Genesis.
But most people are just living to 80.
That's right. There are many reasons for that: wrong lifestyle, poor nutrition, stress, etc. But the most important thing is not if we live to be 80 or even 120 years, but what happens after we die.
So what happens after?
The Bible says that after life comes the judgement and then is the question how we can be free from judgement, how we can be judged to Heaven.
Judgement, it sounds hard.
It can sound hard, but the good news is that God made it possible for you to be declared innocent for everything you've ever done, do you know how?
No, please tell me.
By sending Jesus to us, to take upon Himself everything that makes us guilty, such as impure thoughts, lies, hate, pride, greed, selfishness, jealousy etc.
Hmm...
When we turn away from these things and ask Him to come into our lives, from that moment we will be free from judgement. Do you want that freedom from judgement, forgiveness of all your sin
Absolutely.
May I help you talk to God right now
Yes please.

Diamond
Some things are forever

(Someone is wearing a jewelry that looks like a diamond)
That really looks like a diamond.
Unfortunately, it is not...
They say that diamonds are forever, but do you know what also is forever?
No.
You have a spirit on the inside that will not die when your body dies.
Hmm...
Your spirit will go to God or away from God, and that depends on one thing only.
On what?
If we want to go to God, we must first be forgiven. Forgiven for the things we have opened our lives and hearts for that were not pleasing to Him.
I understand.
Forgiveness for the sins, is given by the one who gave His life for the sins, Jesus Christ. He wants you to turn your heart fully to Him. Do you want to do that?
Absolutely.
When you do this God has something more for you; His Holy Spirit that will help you become the person He created you to be, and to fulfill the destiny He has for your life! Let us pray together.
Yes.

Dice
How good are you?

(Holdng a die)
On a scale of 1-6, how good are you?
A 5, I think.
5 is good, but do you know that we need to be a 6 to go to
Heaven? We need to be perfect to go there.
But no one is perfect, how can we come to Heaven then?
There is one other way, it is to be forgiven, forgiven by the one who came and gave his life for us.
Jesus?
Yes, by His death and resurrection he made it possible for us to call upon Him for forgiveness and salvation. From that moment we belong to God and are on the way to Heaven.
Even those who are as bad as 1 or 2?
Absolutely, forgiveness is available for everybody, God's hand is reached out to the world, but we must with our own free will turn to Him in repentance.
Hmm...
Do you want to be a 6 in God's sight, knowing that you are on the way to Heaven?
Yes, I really want that.
May I help you to talk to God right now?
Sure.

Dirty
Dirty on the inside

(Your friend is wearing a dirty shirt)
Oh, my shirt has become dirty.
You're right, but can I share an important truth with you?
Absolutely.
To be dirty on the outside is a small problem, the real problem is if we are dirty on the inside.
Dirty on the inside?
Yes, when our hearts become dirty with things not pleasing to God. That is the real problem because that closes Heaven for us.
Hmm…
The bad news is that we are all dirty, more or less. The good news is that Jesus came down on the cross and took the 'dirt' upon Himself.
I see.
Today God wants to forgive you, and make your heart clean before
Him. Do you want Him to do that?
Yes.
The Holy Spirit will help you to live a life that God rejoices over and to fulfill your destiny here on earth.
Let us pray together right now. **Sure.**

Divorce
The most terrible divorce

(Somebody is talking about a divorce)
Do you know that it was a divorce that changed the whole world?
Which one was that?
The divorce between man and God.
Are they divorced, what do you mean?
Yes, they are divorced and separated and it was caused by sin in the heart of man.
It does not sound fun.
It is very sad, but don't fear. God is a good God. He loves people, therefore He sent a man to die for the sins of this world. He sent Jesus and because of what He did on the cross, we can come back to God.
Hmm, but what happens if we sin again?
There will always be a fight against sin in our lives. The good news is that God has a gift to us, His Holy Spirit, sent to help you live a life that God rejoices over and to finish your call.
Sounds like a really good gift from Heaven.
It is, and God wants you to experience all this and don't be separated from Him anymore.
I understand.
May I help you talk to God right now?
Please.

Doll
Life is not a toy

(You're see a doll nearby)
A doll is a great toy.
Absolutely, girls love it!
Toys are wonderful to have in life, but many people treat life itself like a toy, and that is very dangerous!
What do you mean?
Life is meant to be really fun and exciting, but it is also serious, because one day we will die and then the Bible says that we have to
stand before God and give account for our lives.
Give account?
Yes, for our lives, how we lived. The bad news is that the things
we have done that were not pleasing to Him, things that broke His commandments, make us guilty before Him. We become criminals in His eyes!
Sounds terrible.
But there is good news also! God did something so that we could be forgiven and stand before Him without fear.
What?
He sent Jesus to be crucified and die. In His death He took all these evil things upon Himself, then He rose again and now He lives forever! When you and I trust Him and call upon Jesus for forgiveness. from that moment we belong to Him, and God will give us the gift of His Spirit. He will help us to know and to do God's will, all the way to Heaven!
Hmm...
I believe it's time for you to get your life right with God. May I help you talk to God right now?
Please do.

Door
Heaven's door is open

(Outside a closed door)
A closed door is not fun.
You are very right.
But the most important thing in life is that Heaven's door is not closed for us.
Heaven's door?
The Bible says that there is a door in Heaven and when life is over it will be either open or closed for us.
What shall we do to have Heaven's door open for us?
We need God's forgiveness, His forgiveness for the things we have done that were not pleasing to Him, the things the Bible calls sin.
Hmm...
When we turn away from these things and put our trust in what Jesus did on the cross, Heaven's door will be opened for us.
I understand.
Do you want His forgiveness and have an open door to Heaven?
Absolutely.
May I help you talk to God right now?
Please.

Doping
We will also be tested

(Watching sports on TV)
Many sportsmen have to face shame when they are caught in the drug test.
Yes, where the truth is revealed!
Do you know that we will undergo a similar test?
What do you mean?
When this life is over, God will examine our lives to see if we are good enough for Heaven.
Hmm...
Heaven is a holy place and no unforgiven sin can enter there. The problem will be if we are tested positive, not for doping, but for unforgiven sin.
I am not a sinner...
If we have lied, stolen, looked with lust or used the Lord's name in vain, we have violated His law and are criminals in His eyes. We'll be tested 'positive for sin', so to speak.
You make me feel guilty...
God has a wonderful solution for that. He provided a Savior 2,000 years ago, who came down on the cross and took our sins upon Himself. What you need to do is repent and trust in Him. Are you ready to do that?
Sure.
Not only will He take your sins away. He will also give you something great. He will fill you with His Holy Spirit, so you can know His will and do it. May I help you talk to God right now?
Absolutely.

Dream
God also has a dream

I dreamt something really nice last night.
(They tell you the dream)
Very interesting, did you know that God also has a dream?
What is that dream about?
He wants everyone to go to Heaven.
I think I'll go there. I'm a quite good person.
It's important to understand that Heaven is a holy place. Heaven is God's place and He decides who can come in there. The problem is called sin, things that are not pleasing to God. If we've not had them forgiven, they will stop us from coming there.
Hmm...
The good news is that God did something so we could be forgiven and escape Hell. Did you know what?
No.
He sent someone to die and take the punishment for sin. His name is Jesus and because of what He did on the cross, we can be forgiven, but there is something we must do.
What?
Welcome Jesus into our lives and with the help of His Spirit, live a life that makes God happy. Do you want to be forgiven and begin a life with God?
Yes, I really want that.
May I help you talk to God right now?
Please do.

Filtered cigarettes
Filter out the impurities

(Your friend is smoking)
Do you know why cigarettes have filters?.
To filter out the poison?
That's right, but did you know that we need a filter in life also?
What do you mean?
A filter that cleanses us from the poison in our lives: impure thoughts, evil words, lies, hate, pride, selfishness, greed, jealousy, etc. Otherwise these things will all be problems on the day we shall try to enter Heaven.
If there is a Heaven...
There is, and God wants you there, but you need to call upon Him to take away the poison in your life.
Hmm...
God sent Jesus to this world to take away the sins and the poison from our hearts. What God wants you to do is to ask Him to be your Lord, and believe in your heart that He took all your sins on the cross. It's not hard for us, but cost Him His life!
It sounds easy.
Don't miss out on Heaven.
No, I don't want to.
Shall we pray?
Yes please.

Fire alarm
We also have an alarm

I see that you have a fire alarm.
Yes, it feels much safer than being without one.
Do you know that we also have an alarm on the inside?
What do you mean?
Our Creator gave us a conscience, and it works like an alarm. It is
God's will, God's law, that is written in our hearts.
Hmm...
When we go against His will and His law, the alarm goes off. We feel bad, we feel guilty. If we steal, lie, hate, lust, are unforgiving, proud or greedy etc, we can feel the alarm going off in our inner being.
You're right.
We need forgiveness for these things, otherwise Heaven's door will be closed for us...
I see.
The good news is that there is forgiveness! Because of what Jesus did on the cross, when He took upon Himself all the things we had done that gave us a bad conscience, all the things we had done that made us guilty before Him! When we turn from sin, to God and put our trust in the Savior, in Jesus and what He did for us on the cross, from that moment we are forgiven and on the way to Heaven.
I understand.
Do you want to receive this forgiveness?
Absolutely.
May I help you talk to God right now?
Please do.

Fishing
Fishers of men

(You are out fishing)
Do you know that one of the first things Jesus said was about fishing?
Is it true?
Yes, He said: 'Follow me and I will make you fishers of men.'
Fishers of men?
Yes, fishers of men to Heaven.
How do you do that?
By helping them understand what we must do to get there.
What must we do to get there?
Turn away from what is not pleasing to God and welcome Jesus into our lives. That is what God wants me and you and everybody else to do.
Hmm...
Heaven is God's gift to you. Now when you know what to do to get there, are you ready to do it?
I think so.
May I help you talk to God right now?
Please do that.

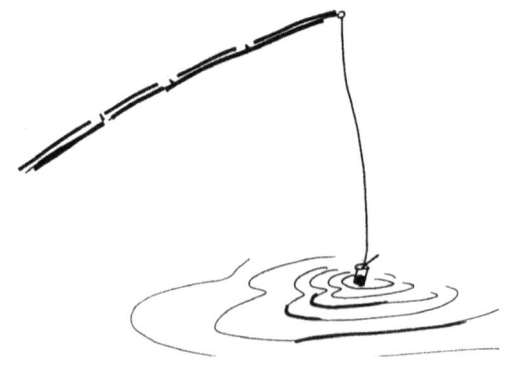

Flight
The whole way to Heaven

Now we're 30,000 feet closer to Heaven.
Ha ha, you're right.
But do you know what we need to do to go the whole way?
Be a good person, I suppose...?
You are right, and a good person according to the Word of God is one who has kept the commandments. How many lies have you told in your life?
I don't know, hundreds maybe... What do you call someone that lies? A liar.
How many things have you taken that did not belong to you?
Many things, but mostly small things.
Small or big, what do you call someone that takes things that don't belong to him?
A thief.
Have you looked upon women and lusted after them?
Every day...
Jesus said that 'if you look upon a woman to lust after her, you commit adultery with her in your heart'.
Hmm...
So by your own admission, you are a lying thief and adulterer at heart, and we have only looked upon three of the commandments. If God judges you by the Ten Commandments, would you be innocent or guilty?
Guilty...
Heaven or Hell?
Hell, I guess.
Does that concern you?
Most definitely.
Do you know what God did, so that you don't have to go to Hell?
No.

He sent Jesus to die and take the punishment for your sins. When we repent and put our trust in Him, we're forgiven.
I understand.
May I help you talk to God right now?
Please do.

Garbage can
A kind of garbage can

(At a garbage can)
Would you like to be a garbage can?
Haha, no thanks. What a strange question.
Actually, there was someone who was a kind of garbage can.
What, explain that?
Perhaps you've heard about Him, Jesus. He was sent to this world to take all the garbage of mankind upon Himself on the cross. He took all the bad things, all the evil things, all the unclean things,
and in that moment He was like garbage can.
It must have been terrible for Him.
It was, but it was important, because man can never go to Heaven with unforgiven garbage in his heart. Jesus made it possible for us to go there.
Hmm...
But there is something we must do and it's not hard for us, but cost Him His life! The Bible describes Him knocking on the door of our lives. When we welcome Him in, then He'll come in and throw out the garbage. From that moment, we're on our way to Heaven. Doesn't that sound great?
It does.
God wants to give you His Holy Spirit too. He will make you the person He wants you to be and help you fulfill your destiny here on earth. Do you want to begin this life today?
Yes, I want that.
May I help you to talk to God?
Yes.

Garbage truck
Give Him your garbage

(Seeing a garbage truck)
Do you know the similarity between a garbage truck and Jesus?
No idea?
He also wants to take our garbage, our sins, the things in our lives that stop us from going to Heaven.
I understand.
Just like we prepare our garbage and put it out in the street, we need to 'give' Him our sins. It doesn't happen automatically, it happens when we ask Him for forgiveness and confess Him as Lord.
Hmm...
Not only does He take away bad things, He also gives us something great! He gives His own Spirit that gives us power to become the person He wants us to be and help us to fulfill our destiny here on earth.
You explain it very well.
Tell me that you want to begin this life today.
Absolutely.
May I help you talk to God right now?
Please do.

Gift
The greatest gift!

(You are giving a gift to a friend)
Thank you so much!
You're welcome. But can I ask you; do you know what the greatest gift anyone has given was?
No idea.
It was when God gave this world Jesus. Sending His only Son to us, to be crucified and to die; taking all the sins of mankind upon Himself.
Hmm...
Jesus is the greatest gift, because He made it possible for us to be forgiven, get back into fellowship with our heavenly Father again and spend eternity in Heaven.
I understand.
But for us to receive this gift, there is something we must do. We must turn away from what the Word of God says is wrong and turn to the Savior, turn to Jesus and welcome Him into our lives. Do you want to receive this gift?
Absolutely.
May I help you talk to God right now?
Yes please.

Globe
He created a perfect world

(Someone is holding a globe)
What a nice globe.
I really like it too.
This world was created perfectly, but something happened. Do you know what?
Please tell me.
Man opened his heart for evil and unclean things and in that same moment man became separated from His Creator.
Hmm...
What followed are all the bad things that we see on earth today.
Yeah, it's terrible!
But there is good news as well!
What?
God did something so that we could be forgiven and come back to Him. He sent a man to die and pay the price for all these sins. When Jesus died on the cross, He opened the way back to God for all of us!
I understand.
God wants you to say 'yes' to this good news by turning your heart and whole life to the Savior, Jesus Christ. Do you want to do that?
Yes, I would really like to.
I will also pray that God gives you His Holy Spirit to help you know His perfect will in every situation and relationship in your life.
Please do that too and let's pray...

Globetrotter
Go into all the world

(Somebody is talking about travelling)
Did you know that Jesus' last words to us, were that we should travel?
Travel where?
He said: 'Go into all the world.'
For what reason?
He said: 'Go into all the world and tell the good news to everybody.' Do you know what the good news is?
Something about God...?
The good news is that there is a Heaven and we can come there.
How can I come there?
It's possible because of what Jesus did for us on the cross, what we need to do is to ask Him to be the Lord of our lives.
I want to do that, but I'm afraid that I will fall back into my old lifestyle after a while.
God will help you with that. He has a gift for us, His Holy Spirit. He will help you and strengthen you to know God's will and to be able to do it. Do you want to experience all this?
Absolutely.
May I help you talk to God right now?
Please do.

GPS
GPS to Heaven

I see that you have a GPS.
Yes, it's a great help many times.
To find the way you mean?
Yes, of course.
But can I ask you, do you have the GPS that shows the way to Heaven?
Ha ha, what do you mean?
I mean, the Bible.
So you are religious?
I would rather say that I have faith; faith in the living God.
I also believe that there must be something out there.
That 'something' is the creator of the world. The bad news is that we are separated from Him because of breaking His law. The Ten Commandments include not lying, stealing, using the Lord's name in vain, lusting etc.
Hmm...
The good news is that Jesus came and took our sins upon Himself. By Him and only by Him we can be forgiven and come to God. Therefore He is 'the way to Heaven'.
I understand.
Do you want to experience forgiveness and begin a relationship with God?
Absolutely.
May I help you talk to God right now?
Please do.

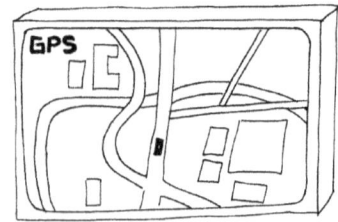

Hammer
The most important tool

(Somebody is having a hammer)
Do you know why the hammer is the most important tool in the world?
Why?
Without it they could not have crucified Jesus and we would still be in our sins, with Heaven closed for us.
Hmm...
They nailed Him to the cross for you and me. Do you know why?
Because of our sins?
You're right, for everything we've done that's not pleasing to God. I received what He did for me many years ago, have you?
Well, I believe in God.
Then you are close! It's important though, that you understand that it is not about believing in something, but receiving someone; receiving Jesus.
No, I have not done that.
Do you want to experience salvation, and say 'yes' to what Jesus did for you on the cross?
Absolutely.
May I help you talk to God right now?
Yes please.

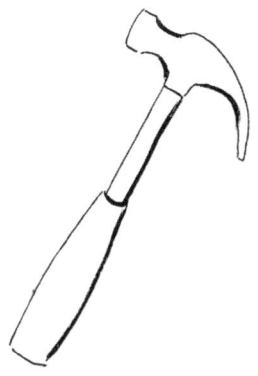

Heaven
The best thing from above

The sky is so beautiful tonight!
Yes, you're right!
Can I ask you a question?
Do you know the worst thing that has come down from the sky?
No, please tell me.
The atomic bombs over Hiroshima and Nagasaki.
Terrible!
But do you know the best thing that has come down from above?
No idea, please tell me.
It was when God sent Jesus to this world from Heaven.
Yes, that must be the best.
Exactly, but what He did on the cross for us when he took upon Himself all the things that had separated God and man, only becomes ours when we do something. Do you know what?
I'm not sure.
When we make a decision in our hearts, to turn away from sin and welcome Jesus Christ into our lives, as our Lord and Savior.
Hmm...
Do you want to say 'yes' to what Jesus did for you on the cross?
I think so.
May I help you talk to God right now?
Please.

High heels
The whole way to Heaven

(Pointing to the lady's shoes)
They're nice; now you're three inches closer to Heaven.
Haha, thank you.
But do you know how to get the whole way to Heaven?
If there is a Heaven, I think we need to be good to go there. Did you know that 'good enough' for God would mean keeping all His commandments? Do you know them?
Well, some of them...
They include not lying, not stealing, not taking the Lord's name in vain, not lusting in our hearts, and that's just four of them! You understand that it's a standard impossible for man to keep...
Hmm...
The bad news is that we are all guilty, the good news is that God made it possible for us to become not guilty!
How?
By sending Jesus to die and to take the sins upon Himself. But we must do something, do you know what?
Please tell me.
Turn away from what is not pleasing to God and receive Jesus
into our lives, from that moment we are on the way to Heaven! Is it anything that hinders you from doing that?
I don't think so.
May I help you talk to God right now?
Absolutly.

Horoscope
My sign is the cross

What star sign are you born in?
In the sign of the cross!
What do you mean?
I'm born again by the blood of Jesus Christ, shed on the cross and I read about my future every day in the Bible. Today it said: 'Surely goodness and love will follow me all the days of my life.'
Your horoscope is the Bible?
No, God forbids using horoscopes. He reveals His will through the Bible and by His Spirit.
Does that work for you?
Yes, and it will work for you too!
It sounds like a fairy tale to me.
God wants to show you that He is real and that Jesus is the way to Him. It all begins with you being open and honest with God and asking Him to show you what's right and true.
Well, I have always had an open heart. Wonderful to hear, may I pray for you right now? Yes.

House
Heaven is God's house

(Visiting a friend)
I really like your house.
Thank you, I like it too.
Am I right when I say that you decide who can come in here?
Totally right.
Would you let someone in here, to live with you, that you did not know, that was very very dirty.
Haha, I don't think so...
It's the same with Heaven, it is God's house, and He decides who can come in or not.
Hmm...
The problem is if we are dirty with unforgiven sin. Dirty and guilty by breaking His commandments; with impure thought, lies, hate, pride, envy, greed, selfishness, unforgiveness, indifference etc.
I understand.
The good news is that God wants everybody to go to Heaven and has made it possible. Do you know how?
No, please tell me.
By sending a man to die for our sins, so that we could be forgiven and clean and enter Heaven. His name is Jesus.
Hmm...
What we need to do is to turn away from our sin and welcome Jesus into our lives. From that moment, Heaven's door will be open for us. Do you want to begin that life today?
I think so.
May I pray for you right now?
Please do.

Ingredients
God knows what's inside

Do you usually check the ingredients?
Almost never...
I know someone that always does.
Who is that?
God, and He will read our table of contents the day we stand before Him to see if we have what it takes to come to Heaven.
Who can enter Heaven?
The one who's sin has been forgiven. Sin is not only rape and murder, but also impure thoughts, lies, hate, pride, greed, jealousy, selfishness, unforgiveness, bitterness, etc. Sin is a big problem for all of us...
I understand. Who can enter Heaven then?
Only those who have received Jesus and the forgiveness of their sins. Do you know how we receive forgiveness?
Ask for forgiveness?
God sent a man to this world, to be crucified and die for our sins, He sent Jesus and because of what He did on the cross, we can be forgiven. What we need to do is to turn away from what we know is not pleasing to God and put our trust in Jesus.
Hmm...
From that moment we are forgiven and the day we stand before God, we will be welcomed into Heaven. Do you want this forgiveness that God is offering you?
Yes.
God's Spirit will help you to live the life that is pleasing to Him, so that you don't have to fight and struggle by yourself. **Sounds really good.** May I help you talk to God right now?
Please do.

TABLE OF CONTENTS

Impure thoughts	95.342
Lies	27.218
Hate	5.331
Pride	11.619
Greed	996
Envy	5.318
Stealing	524
Unforgiveness	413

Injured
The relationship is injured

(Somebody is walking on crutches) What has happened?
My ankle was injured during a baseball game.
I hope you will get well soon, my friend. But do you know what is 'injured' more?
What do you mean?
The relationship with our Creator. It is 'injured' because we have opened our lives for wrong things.
Hmm...
But the good news is that God did something so that the relationship could be healed again.
Tell me!
He became one of us, He became a man in the person Jesus
Christ. He died on the cross for all the things we had done that had
'injured' the relationship with our Creator!
I believe that.
Great, the next step for you is to welcome Him personally into your life. Do you want to do that?
Yes.
Let us pray together then.

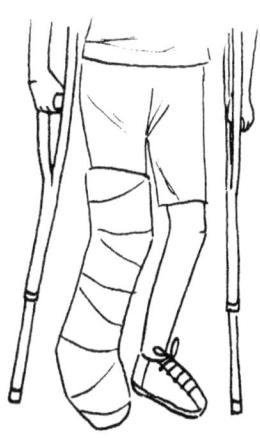

Insurance
The most important insurance

(In your friend's house)
Do you have insurance in case a fire breaks out in your house?
Of course, it would be a catastrophe otherwise.
You're right, but there is a much more important insurance, do you know what that is?
No, please tell me.
The insurance that takes us to Heaven when we die.
What kind of insurance is that?
It is a person, Jesus Christ! Because of what He did on the cross, when He took all the sins of the world, He is able to forgive the sins, so that nothing will stop us from going to Heaven.
…and…
We need to be 'insured' so that it won't be a catastrophe when we die, because it will be, if we die with our sins unforgiven.
Hmm…
What we need to do is to turn away from what the Word of God says is wrong and turn to Jesus and welcome Him into our lives. From that day we are 'insured'. Do you want to have this 'insurance' in your life?
Of course.
May I help you talk to God right now?
Yes please.

Jewelry
You are a treasure

That is a very nice jewelry you have!
Thank you, I like it too.
But do you know that all of you are a jewelry, a treasure?
Haha, thank you!
Perhaps not in everybody's eyes, but in God's eyes!
Hmm...
First he made a wonderful world for you to live in, then He did something fantastic again, do you know what?
I'm not really sure...
He gave you a Savior! He sent a man to this world to die, so that you could be forgiven, have peace with God and go to Heaven!
I understand.
But you need to say 'yes' to this gift; you do that by saying 'goodbye' to sin and welcome Jesus Christ personally into your life. Do you want to do that today?
I think so.
May I help you talk to God right now?
Sure.

Key
The most important key

Are these your keys?
Yes, they are mine.
Are they important to you?
Enormously important.
I see, but do you have the most important key?
What key do you mean?
They key to Heaven.
They key to Heaven?
Yes, that key is a person, and His name is Jesus. The things we have done that are not pleasing to God have locked Heaven for us, and we can never lock it up ourselves, with our own goodness. We need His goodness, His sacrifice on the cross.
I don't care so much about what happens after I'm dead... You should, your spirit will go somewhere when life here is over. There is nothing more important than your eternal salvation! Hmm...
This is good news my friend. God offers you the key to Heaven, the key to eternal life.
Continue.
Do you know what you must do to get this key?
No, please tell me.
Turn to God, and trust in Jesus' sacrifice on the cross as the key for your eternal life. Welcome Him as Lord.
I think I'll do that some time.
May I help you talk to God right now?
Please do.

Ladder
The ladder to Heaven

(Your friend has been on a ladder)
Now you've been a little closer to Heaven.
Haha, you're right.
But do you know how to get the whole way there?
I have to die?
That's usually true, but please don't die without having your sins forgiven! Unforgiven sins are a big problem, because we can't enter Heaven with them in our lives.
Hmm...
That was the bad news; the good news is that God did something for us, so that we could have all our sins forgiven. Do you know what?
Please tell me.
He sent His Son to die on a cross, and on the cross He took the punishment for all sin and evil.
So that's what it's all about...
If what Jesus did on the cross shall be relevant to us, we need to do something as well. We need to repent from our sins and turn to God and trust that what Jesus did on the cross is enough for Him to forgive all our sins. Do you want to say yes to what Jesus did for you?
I think so.
May I pray for you right now?
Please do.

Law
God also has a law

(Somebody is mentioning a crime)
If we break the law, and are caught, we must pay the penalty.
That's right.
Did you know that God also has a law?
He does?
Yes. Have you heard about The Ten Commandments?
Of course...
If we break them, we have to pay the penalty.
What is the penalty?
It's a tough penalty - missing Heaven!
That is tough...
Heaven is a holy place, Heaven is God's 'house' and no one will come in with unforgiven lies, theft, hate, pride, envy, greed, lust, selfishness, bitterness, etc.
How can we get to Heaven then?
God sent someone to this world who took all these sins upon Himself. His name is Jesus. Through faith in Him, we reach Heaven, but if we deny Him, we remain in our sin.
But I'm young. I can think about this later.
You have no guarantee for later; your life can end tomorrow.
I understand.
God wants to give you forgiveness and salvation. Do you want to experience that?
Yes.
May I help you talk to God right now?
Yes please.

Lifebuoy
Grab the lifebuoy!

(At a lake or river)
Would you be thankful if someone tried to save your life if you were drowning?
Very.
When someone is drowning, you throw him a lifebuoy. In the same way God sent Jesus to rescue us from drowning in our sins.
I'm not a big sinner.
As it's written in the Psalms: 'If you Lord, kept a record of sins, who could stand?'
What does that mean?
If God would keep a record of every time we've been thinking impure thoughts; every time we have been using our mouth to speak evil words or lies; every time when we have been taking something that did not belong to us; every time we have been proud, jealous, greedy, selfish, unforgiving, indifferent, we would all stand very guilty before Him.
I understand.
But God did something so that we should not have to stand guilty before Him. Do you know what?
No.
He sent His lifebuoy; He sent Jesus, to be crucified, to die and in that way paid the price for our sins. God wants you to grab that lifebuoy!
How do I do that?
By turning to God and asking Jesus to be the Lord and Savior of your life. Do you want to do that?
Absolutely.
May I help you talk to God right now?
Please do.

Lost
Find the way to Heaven

(Somebody is lost or can't find their way)
I will help you, but the most important thing is to know the way to
Heaven.
What do you mean?
I mean, if you know what you need to do to go to Heaven.
Being a nice and loving person, I suppose...
That's good; the problem is the bad things we've done; the things not pleasing to God. Without them being forgiven, they will hinder us from entering into Heaven.
Hmm...
The good news is that God sent a man into this world nearly 2,000 years ago, who took our sins upon Himself. His name is Jesus and He made it possible for us to be forgiven and go to Heaven.
I understand.
But we don't go to Heaven automatically, there is something we must do.
What?
Believe in Jesus and trust God to empower you with His Spirit to live a life that is pleasing to Him. Do you want to do that?
Now?
The sooner, the better.
Okay.
May I help you talk to God right now?
Please.

Lost and found
What we have all lost

(Great at trains, flights or buses)
I saw that they have a 'lost and found' department here.
Yes, that's normal.
That's very good if we lose something, but did you know what's the most important thing that all people lose and most people don't even know about it?
I have no idea...
It is our innocence before God, our right standing before Him.
What do you mean, have we all lost that?
When we were born, we were born belonging to God. We had never done anything wrong, we could not distinguish right from wrong or good from evil. The problem came as we grew up and opened our hearts for bad things, wrong things and evil things...
Hmm...
In that moment, when sin entered our hearts, we lost the relationship with God, we were separated from Him. This happens to everybody. No one can live a life that in God's eyes are perfect without God's help. The problem is that if we die separated from Him, we'll miss Heaven.
So what shall we do?
The good news is that God did something standing with Him again. He sent a man, He sent Jesus, to be crucified and to die and to take upon Himself all the things that we had done th had separated us and our Creator!
I believe in Jesus.

It's great, next step for you is to welcome Him into your life, as your personal Lord and Savior. May I pray together with you right now?
Please do!

Lunch
Taking Heaven for granted

(You are having lunch with a friend)
Many people put salt on the food before they taste it.
Yes, I have seen that.
They take for granted that the chef has forgotten the salt.
Haha.
But do you know the most dangerous thing that people take for granted?
No idea?
That they will go to Heaven because they are good.
But most people are good...
According to our standard, yes, but according to God's standard, no! God's requirement for entrance to Heaven is to have kept the commandments. Never lying, stealing, hating, looking with lust, using the Lord's name in vain etc... When we examine ourselves according to this standard we'll soon understand that we are not good, but dirty and guilty before God!
You make me feel condemned...
The good news is that God made it possible for us to get our sins away; do you know how?
By sending Jesus to us?
Yes, that's right, and He did His part when He died on the cross. Now we must do our part. Do you know what that is?
Not exactly...
It is to say goodbye to what is not pleasing to God and to welcome the Savior Jesus Christ into our lives. Are you open to do that?
I think so...
May I help you talk to God right now?
Yes.

Make up
Beautiful on the inside

Your make up is very nice today.
Thank you.
But there is only one way to be beautiful on the inside.
How?
By recieving forgivness for everything we have done that were not pleasing to God
Hmm...
Forgivness is possible because Jesus Christ came down on the cross and died for the sins of the world.
I understand
When we turn away from what the Word of God says is wrong, and turn to Jesus, He will come into our lives and make a total make- over on the inside of us. This is for you, do you want to experience this make-over?
Absolutely
May I help you talk to God right now?
Yes, please

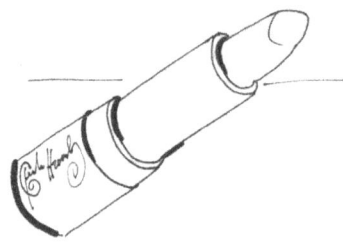

Map
The most important map

(Somebody is looking at a map)
Can I ask you something?
What?
Do you have the most important map?
What map do you mean?
The map to Heaven - the Bible!
Well, I have one at home.
But have you read it?
Yes, parts of it.
Then you know the way to Heaven?
Well, it has something to do with believing, right?
Jesus is the way to Heaven. Believe in God and welcome Jesus into your life as your Lord and Savior. Trust that what He suffered on the cross was enough to forgive you your sins, all the things you've done that separate you from God.
I understand.
He's the Savior; the one who saves us from our sins, but also opens the way for you to receive God's Spirit into your life. The Spirit will help you understand 'the map' and follow it. Do you want the Savior of the world to be your Lord?
Absolutely.
May I help you talk to God right now?
Please do.

Medicine
The most important medicine

(Noticing when someone is taking their medicine)
I see that you take medicine.
Yes, it's for my allergies.
But have you taken the most important medicine?
What do you mean?
There is a medicine that takes away sin and evil from our lives, so that we can go to Heaven.
What is that?
It is a person and His name is Jesus. When He died on the cross, when He took upon Himself all the things we had done that separated God and us, in that moment, He became like a medicine.
Hmm...
When we turn to Him, put our trust in Him and welcome Him into our lives; from that moment He forgives us, removes our sins and connects us with God.
I understand.
Do you want to receive the medicine that God offers you?
I think so.
God also has another wonderful gift. His Holy Spirit that helps us to become the person God wants us to be. He is our Helper to fulfill our destiny here on earth.
Interesting.
May I help you talk to God right now?
Please.

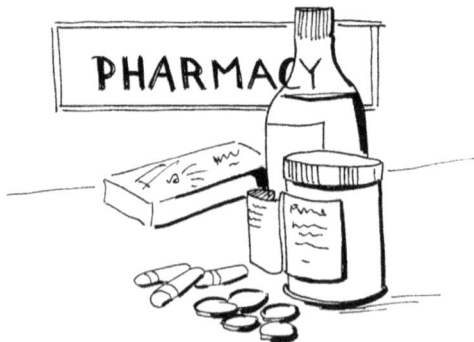

Mirror
The Bible and the mirror

(In front of a mirror)
Do you know the difference between a mirror and the Bible?
Hmm, no idea.
In the mirror we see if we can go out, in the Bible we see if we can come in, to Heaven.
But I'm a good person, I'm quite sure I will go to Heaven. Even if we think we are good, we need to see God's standard for what is good; good enough for Heaven.
Good enough?
Yes, God's standard is The Ten Commandments. You shall not lie, you shall not steal, you shall not take the Lord's name in vain and so on, and Jesus made it even sharper when He talked about God examining our very thoughts.
Hmm...
So the day we die and stand before God we will all be in big trouble, if we do not have the Savior. The good news is that He is ready to take all our sins away; His name is Jesus.
I believe in Jesus.
That's a good beginning; the next step is to invite Him to be the Lord of your life and receive salvation personally. Do you want His forgiveness and to begin a relationship with God?
I think so...
May I help you talk to God right now?
Please do.

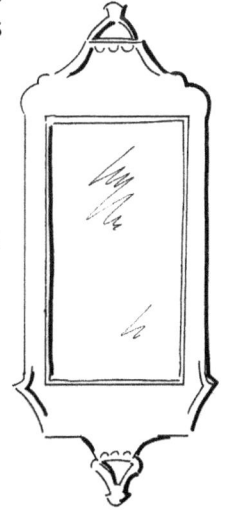

Missing People
Are you missing?

(In front of a 'missing people' notice)
It is heartbreaking to see these missing people notices.
Yes, really.
But do you know that there also is a 'missing people list' in Heaven?
What do you mean?
God also has a 'missing people list', and one of the persons on that list is you.
Me, what do you mean?
When you were born you belonged to God, but as you grew up and opened your life and heart for things that were not pleasing to Him, you and He became separated.
Hmm...
This happens to everyone of us. We are separated from our Creator because of sin. The good news is that God is a good God; He wants us back. Otherwise we are missing from His family.
I understand.
The sins must be removed. They must be forgiven and that was the reason God sent Jesus. When He died on the cross, He took upon Himself all the things we had done that had separated our Creator and us! When He rose again, He became the Savior of the world, the only one able to forgive sin!
I believe this.
The next step for you is to turn away from all evil deeds and thoughts and turn to Jesus, asking Him to become Lord and Savior of your life. May I pray together with you right now?
Please do.

Mistake
The biggest mistake

(Someone is using the word 'mistake')
Do you know what would be our biggest mistake?
No...
To miss Heaven.
Heaven? I am not religious.
This is not about religion, this is about what will happen when life here is over. It's about where we will spend eternity.
Eternity? Do you really believe that man lives forever?
The Bible makes clear that when a man dies, His spirit leaves his body and goes somewhere.
Hmm...
Because God wants everyone to come to Heaven, He made it easy for us to get there. Do you know how?
I'm not sure.
By turning away from evil and welcoming Jesus into our lives. That is what God requires of man.
I understand.
Don't do the biggest mistake a man can do and miss Heaven because of unforgiven sin, when Jesus paid the price for total forgiveness. Don't play with your eternity.
You've really given me something to think about.
May I pray for you right now?
Please.

Money
Rich in many ways

(Somebody is talking about a rich person)
We can be rich in many different ways.
What do you mean?
You can be materially rich with much money, friends, health, knowledge, but the most important thing is to be spiritually rich.
What do you mean by that?
It is when you are on the way to Heaven.
I was born Catholic.
It's a good beginning, but it's also important to understand the difference between believing in something and receiving someone; receiving the living Savior.
I'm not sure that I understand.
It is when we have turned away from what we know is not pleasing to God, received forgiveness by faith in what Jesus did on the cross and welcome Him into our lives as Lord, that we are on the way to Heaven.
Hmm...
God made Heaven for you and He wants you there, but this is what you must do first. Do you understand?
I do.
God's Spirit will give you strength and wisdom to know His will and do it, so that you can fulfill your destiny in reaching out to your generation.
Very good.
Do you want to begin this life today?
Absolutely.
May I help you talk to God right now?
Please.

National anthem
Land of the free

(The American national anthem is playing)
We have a great national anthem.
You're right, I really like it.
It tells about the land of the free.
Yes.
It is wonderful with freedom in a nation, but do you know what's the most important freedom?
From fear perhaps?
Not only from fear, but to be free from sin; because unforgiven sin stops us from going to Heaven.
Hmm...
The good news is that God provided a Savior 2,000 years ago. When Jesus died on the cross, He paid the price for sin. When He rose again He became the Savior of the world with authority to forgive sins. Do you know what to do to receive that forgiveness?
Ask for it?
What we need to do, according to the Bible, is to repent and trust in Christ. Do you want to do that?
Absolutely.
He will set you totally free today. May I help you talk to God right now?
Please do.

National Independence day
Celebrating our most important day

Soon we'll celebrate our Nation's Independence Day.
Yes, that is always fun!
What day in your life do you celebrate the most?
Definitely my birthday, the day I was born.
Do you know what day I celebrate the most? Not the day I was born, but the day I was born again! The day I turned to God.
Hmm...
Our birthday is really a day to celebrate; but the day we turn to God, receive forgiveness and get assurance of Heaven is the best day in our lives!
I believe in God.
That is a good beginning. The next step is to welcome Jesus Christ into your life as your Lord and Savior, and God will give you the gift of His Spirit. He will help you to know and to do God's will. Then
you can be sure that you belong to God and are on the way to
Heaven!
I understand.
God wants this date to be your spiritual birthday. Today is a perfect day to come to God!
Okay.
Shall we pray together?
Yes please.

News
The greatest news

(Someone is reading the newspaper)
What do you think should be the greatest news in the world?
I don't know.
It should be that there is a Heaven and that we can come there.
It would be fantastic news!
The good news is that it is true. The Word of God speaks much about Heaven and that it is possible for us to go there, but there is something we must do.
What, believe?
We must receive the one God sent to this world into our lives, we must receive Jesus.
Jesus? But I am a Muslim.
My friend, this is not about religion. The Creator of the world sent a man to this place to die for the sins of man, the sins we had done that separated Him and us. He sent Jesus to 'bridge the gap' that sin had created.
Hmm...
We need to respond and say yes to what He did for us, whether we are born in America, Europe, Africa or Asia, it is the same for everyone.
I understand.
The next step for you is to welcome Jesus into your life, and I promise that He will show Himself real to you.
You have given me something to think about.
May I pray for you?
Please.

'No smoking'
Sin is more dangerous!

(At a 'no smoking' sign)
Don't you think it's strange that there is never any 'sin forbidden' sign?
Haha, what do you mean?
It is so much more dangerous.
Explain...
Smoking shortens our lives, but sin makes us miss Heaven.
Miss Heaven?
That's right, Heaven is God's place and no one living in sin can enter there.
Hmm...
So we must be forgiven, we must get the sins away. The good news is that it is possible, it is possible because of what Jesus did for us, when He took the punishment of sin on the cross.
I believe that.
It's a good beginning, now you need to welcome Him into your life, as your Lord and Savior, that is what takes people to Heaven.
I understand.
God also wants to give you His Holy Spirit, so that it will be easy for you to say no to sin and live the life God has for you. Do you want to begin this life today?
I think so.
May I help you talk to God right now?
Please.

One way street
One way to Heaven

(Driving with a friend) This is a one way street.
Yes.
Did you know that there's a 'one way street' to Heaven as well?
What do you mean?
Jesus said: 'No one can come to the Father but through me.' We cannot come to God any other way. If we try, it's like travelling the wrong directions on a one way street. Sooner or later we will crash!
Hmm...
The good news is that the way is open. God is waiting for us, to turn away from our sins and follow Jesus.
I think I understand.
More good news is that God wants to give you His Holy Spirit to help you fulfill the destiny He has for you here on earth! Do you want to experience this?
Absolutely.
May I help you talk to God right now?
Yes please.

Parking ticket
He paid your fine

Do you think the owner of this car would be happy if someone took this note and paid the fine?
Yes, very happy.
That is what Jesus did when He died on the cross. He paid the price for our sins.
Continue...
The Bible tells us that the wages of sin is death, so somebody had to die, somebody that was without sin, to be able to 'pay our fine'.
Sounds complicated.
It is not, God created a perfect world, this perfect world was destroyed by man's sin, but Jesus came and paid the price for sin.
Hmm...
He made is possible for us to be forgiven, be connected with God and go to Heaven, and God wants to take your 'fine' also!
My fine?
Yes, the fine you have to pay for the things you have done that were not pleasing to Him, these things make you guilty before Him and closes Heaven. Do you know what to do?
No, please tell me.
Turn away from what the Bible says is wrong and welcome Jesus into your life. From that moment He takes your fine and you are on the way to Heaven.
Sounds good.
May I help you talk to God right now?
Please do.

Peace sign
Peace with God

(Somebody is carrying a 'peace sign')
I see that you are wearing a 'peace sign'.
Yes, my dream is a world without war, a world in peace.
I totally agree with you, but there is a peace that is more important than the peace between nations...
What peace do you mean?
I mean the peace we can have with our Creator, the peace we can have in our hearts, knowing that we belong to Him and that we are on the way to Heaven.
Hmm...
The bad news is that we have all done things that destroyed that peace. The good news is that God sent Jesus to die for these things. When we make a decision to live a life that makes God happy and welcome the Savior, welcome Jesus into our lives, from that moment we have peace with God and we are on the way to Heaven!
I understand.
God loves the fact that you want peace on Earth, but He also wants you to have peace with Him. He wants to give you that peace today. Do you want to receive it?
Absolutely.
May I help you talk to God right now?
Please.

Peter
Peter: The Rock

(You're meeting someone named Peter)
Did you know that your name means 'The Rock'?
Yes, I have heard that.
Do you know where that comes from?
I have no idea.
In the Bible there is a passage when Jesus asks Peter who He is. Peter answers; 'You are the Messiah, the Son of the living God'. Then Jesus says; 'On this rock, I will build my church'.
Interesting.
The rock was not Peter, but something that Peter had said: 'You are the Son of the living God'.
I understand.
God wants you to believe that also, and to tell Him that you trust that Jesus died on the cross for you. The day you do that and mean it, you are on the way to Heaven!
Hmm...
May I help you talk to God right now?
Yes, would you please?

Police
God is not a policeman

(You see a policeman or police car)
Many people look at God like a policeman.
What do you mean?
Like He is the police of the Universe, always ready to punish any disobedience, but that is a very, very wrong picture of God.
So what is the right picture?
The Bible speaks about Him as a good and loving Father. A Father who wants His children to have a great life here and after that go to Heaven.
It sounds like you have been brainwashed.
No, but I have been washed in my heart from all evil and unclean things that stopped me from going to Heaven. There is only one that can do that, the one that God sent to us, the one who was crucified for these things, His name is Jesus.
Hmm...
When He died on the cross, He also died for you, so that you could be washed totally clean and stand innocent before God when this life is over.
You really believe in this...
With my whole heart, I know that God is real.
You have given me something to think about.
May I talk to God for you?
Absolutely.

Quote
My favorite quote

(Someone tells their favorite quote)
Do you want to hear my favorite quote?
No, tell me!
It was the last thing Jesus said: 'Go into all the world and tell the good news to everybody!'
So that was the last He said?
Yes, do you know what the good news He was talking about is?
About peace on earth perhaps?
No, the good news He was talking about is that there is a Heaven and that we can come there.
Yes, I really believe that all good people will go there.
Well, that's not totally correct. Heaven is a holy place, Heaven is where God lives and no one living in sin can enter that place. But because of what Jesus did for us on the cross we can be forgiven of our sins and nothing will stop us from going to Heaven.
Hmm...
What God wants us to do is turn away from what the Bible says is not pleasing to God and put our trust in the Savior, in Jesus. Then we will go to Heaven.
Have you done that?
Many years ago, now it is your turn, I can help you if you want.
Please.

Recipe
The recipe for eternal life

(Somebody is talking about a recipe)
Do you know that there is a recipe for eternal life?
Is it?
Yes, in the Bible it says: 'This is eternal life: that they may know you the only true God, and Jesus Christ whom you have sent.'
I agree totally, I believe that also, but I don't like the church rules that I can't drink, dance or have sex with my girlfriend. Doesn't God want us to be happy?
When we welcome Jesus into our lives, things will happen. His Holy Spirit will come in and live on the inside of us and form us to the person He wants us to be.
Please continue...
I can compare it by buying new beautiful clothes. We love to wear them and the old become uninteresting. Your relationship with God, and your will to make Him happy will be most interesting to you.
Hmm...
We can never come to God and learn to know Him if we live the way we want, we must play after His rules. He wants to see a surrendered heart in us, a heart that wants to follow Him in everything.
I understand.
Are you ready to come to God His way, which is the holy way?
I think so.
May I pray with you?
Sure.

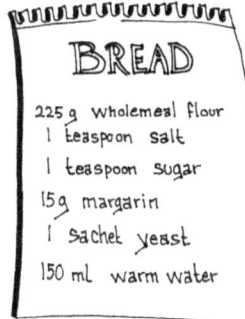

BREAD
225 g wholemeal flour
1 teaspoon salt
1 teaspoon sugar
15 g margarin
1 sachet yeast
150 ml warm water

Replay
Our lives in replay

(A replay is on TV)
Do you know that our lives will go in replay?
What do you mean?
When this life is over and we stand before God he will go through our lives again.
How do you know that? Well, it is what the Bible says. Hmm...
It will be a very special day but do you know what the problem is?
No...
The problem is the bad things we have done, the things the Bible calls sin, such as impure thoughts, evil words and lies, envy, greed, selfishness, unforgiveness, indifference etc. With these things unforgiven, we can never enter Heaven!
I understand.
That is the bad news, the good news is that God had a plan to take away the sins. That plan was Jesus Christ crucified. He sent His Son to this world to take upon Himself all the things we had in our lives that stopped us from going to Heaven.
Hmm...
He did His part 2,000 years ago, now we must do our part, do you know what that is?
Be a good person?
There are two things we need to do, first turn away from what the Word of God says is wrong, then to welcome Jesus into our lives as our Savior. Do you want to do that?
Absolutely.
May I help you talk to God right now?
Please do.

Ring
The most important relationship

I see that you have a very important relationship. (Pointing at the ring)

That's right, I've been married for two years.

Congratulations, but do you know the most important relationship? (Pointing towards Heaven)

Well, I believe in God.

It's a good beginning, but our lives with God shall be much like our lives with our partner. It's not about believing, but about fellowship.

I'm not there in my life with God.

It's no problem, the way to God is open for every man, because of what Jesus did for us on the cross. With that act, He made it possible for us to be forgiven. Forgiven of the things that cannot be in God's presence.

Hmm...

When you make a decision to make Jesus Lord and welcome him into your life, your fellowship with God begins, and you can be sure of Heaven. This is for you!

Definitely.

May I pray with you?

Yes please.

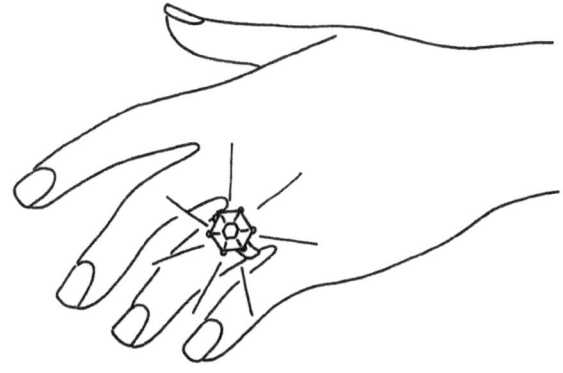

Scale
Good deeds are not enough

(Somebody is talking about their weight)
Do you know what we shall never put on a scale but most people tend to do?
No idea.
Our good deeds and hope they are good enough for Heaven.
Doesn't God like good deeds?
Yes, but the question is not if we have done enough good deeds, but if we have had any bad deeds, any sins, because people with unforgiven sins can't enter Heaven.
Everybody sins...
You are right, it is impossible for humans to live perfect lives. That means a big problem for us, the day we die and God judges us.
Hmm...
The good news is that God knew that man needed a Savior, somebody that would take the sins upon Himself. So He sent His only Son, He sent Jesus to be crucified and die, taking the punishment of sin upon Himself.
I believe that.
Great, next step for you is to ask Jesus to be your personal Lord and Savior. Then God's Holy Spirit will help you to know God's will and do it. Do you want to experience that?
I think so.
May I help you talk to God right now?
Please do.

Security check
Some things can't enter

(At the airport)
Do you know it will be like this when we shall enter Heaven?
What do you mean?
There are things in our lives that never can enter Heaven.
Like...?
Impure thoughts, evil words, lies, hate, pride, envy, selfishness, greed, unforgiveness, indifference etc. The Bible calls them sins, and this means a big problem for all of us.
Yes, no one will pass through that standard...
You're right, when we compare ourselves with other people, we can look quite good, but when we compare with God's standard we will all stand guilty.
Hmm...
The good news is that God sent a man to this world, to die for our sins, this man is Jesus. When we turn to Him for forgiveness, He will take away everything in our lives that stops us from going to Heaven.
It was really good news.
God wants you to receive that forgiveness today, and it's very easy. Call upon Jesus from an honest heart, from that moment you are forgiven and will pass through the gate of Heaven without any problem! **Would be great.**
May I help you talk to God right now?
Absolutely.

Shower
Clean on the inside

(In the shower at the gym)
Nice with a warm shower.
Yeah, I agree.
I once had a shower that changed my life. I had my conscience washed clean from all guilt and shame.
How did that happen?
I put my trust in what Jesus did for me when He died on the cross and asked Him to become Lord of my life. Then I experienced for the first time how I became completely clean on the inside and the peace of God which is beyond description.
Interesting.
Yeah, and God wants everyone to have that peace, including you.
Hmm...
What God wants you to do is to trust that what Jesus did on the cross was also for you. Do you want to have this peace and washing on the inside too?
I think so.
May I help you talk to God now?
Absolutely.

Smiley
Most happy over

(Someone is wearing a 'smiley button')
I see that you are wearing a 'smiley button'.
Yes, I think that we shall be happy and think about all the good things we have.
I totally agree! Can I ask what you are most happy with in your life?
Oh, many things, especially my family and friends!
Do you know what I am most happy with?
No, please tell me.
That someone made it possible for me to go to Heaven!
What do you mean?
When God sent His son to die on the cross, He took upon Himself all the things that stop us from going to Heaven. Lies, hate, stealing, pride, greed, jealousy, lust, selfishness, unforgiveness etc. He took it all!
Hmm...
When we turn away from these things and welcome Jesus as Lord into our lives, from that moment we are on the way to Heaven. Do you want to do that?
I think so...
God will also give you His Holy Spirit, who will help you to become the person He wants you to be. He will help you to fulfill your destiny here on earth. May I help you talk to God right now?
Please do.

Snow
White as snow

(Making a heart in the snow)
Our hearts need to be white as snow to enter Heaven.
Then I am in bad trouble...
We are all in bad trouble, because it is impossible to live such a perfect life. But don't fear, there is some good news also!
What?
God knew that no one could live a perfect life and go to Heaven by Himself, but because He wanted man to go there, He sent a man to us. He sent Jesus to die for the sins of the world so that we could be forgiven, receive a heart white as snow, stand innocent before God, and be sure of Heaven.
It really sounds like good news!
A good God comes with good news, but there is something we must do to receive this. God wants us to turn away from what we know is wrong and welcome Jesus into our lives. Do you want to do that?
I think so.
May I help you talk to God right now?
Yes please.

Substitute
He became our substitute

(In a classroom with a substitute teacher)
We have a substitute today.
I see, I hope they've called for a good one this time...
Yes, I hope so too, but do you know who was the most important substitute in history?
No idea.
It was Jesus Christ. When God sent Him to be crucified and to die, He became our substitute. He payed the price for sin instead of us, He suffered instead of us, He died instead of us.
I don't really understand...
Sin is always punished, when we break God's commandments there is a punishment. The penalty for sin is death. The good news is that God is a good God. He loves people and He doesn't want
us to be punished. He wanted us to be forgiven.
I understand.
So He punished Jesus instead of us. When Jesus died on the cross He took upon Himself all the things that we had done that deserved punishment, all the things we had done that made us guilty before Him. We shall be very happy for that!
Indeed!
What we need to do is to receive what Jesus did for us so that we can be forgiven, to believe that He died for our sins and rose again. When we do that and welcome Him into our lives as our Lord and Savior, we are on the way to Heaven.
Hmm...
Do you want Him to be your substitute?
Absolutely.
May I help you talk to God right now?
Please do.

Synagogue
The Jewish Congregation

(Outside the synagogue)
Do you know what kind of building this is?
Some kind of church?
No, it's a synagogue; a congregation place for Jews.
Aha!
Do you know why most Jews don't believe that Jesus was the Messiah?
No idea?
They waited for a king, but the Bible talks about that Jesus first would come as a servant and die, but the second time He would come as a king and reign.
I understand.
When he died, He died for us, do you know why?
For the sins?
Yes, because no one living in sin can enter Heaven. First we must have the sins forgiven and cleansed away. Do you know how?
Not exactly. Can I tell you? Absolutely.
What you need to do is to put your trust in Jesus. Ask Him to become the Lord of you life. God's Holy Spirit will help you to continue to walk with Him and do His will. Do you want to experience this?
Of course.
May I help you talk to God right now?
Please do.

Tattoo
Beautiful on the inside

(Somebody has a tattoo)
What is the history behind that tattoo?
(They are answering)
Interesting. Many people try to make their body beautiful with tattoos, but there is only one way to make our hearts beautiful. **How?**
By inviting Jesus Christ into our lives as Lord. When He comes in, He cleanses our hearts, makes them beautiful and ready for Heaven!
Hmm...
Heaven is a Holy place and we will only be welcomed there if our hearts are made clean by the Savior; if we receive forgiveness from God.
I believe in life after death.
Great. The next step is for you to turn away from sin and turn to your Savior. May I help you talk to God right now?
Absolutely.

Ticket
The ticket to Heaven

(On a bus or train)
To where is your ticket?
L.A.
Okay, but do you have the most important ticket, the ticket to
Heaven?
What do you mean?
There are tickets to geographical places, but there is also a ticket to Heaven and that is the most important ticket and it's already paid for.
What do you mean with that?
When Jesus died on the cross, He died for the consequences of our sins, He paid the price for the whole mankind to be forgiven and get this ticket to Heaven, for those who take it by faith.
I don't deny that there is a God.
It's good, but you need to make Jesus the Lord of your life to get this ticket. Do you want this ticket?
It's for me.
May I help you talk to God right now?
Please do.

Tie
On the way up

(You meet someone with a tie)
Your tie is really nice!
Thank you very much.
I like ties. There is only one thing that I don't like about them; that they point downward; because I am not going down, I am on the way up, to Heaven! Do you know where you are going?
Up, I hope...
You need to be sure. The Word of God says that when we repent and put our trust in what Jesus Christ did for us on the cross; from that moment we belong to God and are on the way to Heaven!
I believe in God.
That's great. The next step is to make Jesus the Lord of your life; He will also give you His Holy Spirit that will help you fulfill your destiny here on earth.
I understand.
Let us pray together right now.
Sure.

Traffic light
Green light to Heaven

(You're sitting at a stop light with a friend)
Do you prefer red or green lights?
Green, of course.
Would you prefer a red or a green light to Heaven?
Green of course.
But do you know how to get a green light?
Be a good person, I suppose?
Many people think so. The problem is the bad things we have done; the things that are not pleasing to God. If we try to enter Heaven without these things being forgiven, we'll find ourselves facing red light.
Aha...
The good news is that God is ready to forgive us for all these things, and give us the green light to Heaven. This happens when we put out trust in what Jesus did for us on the cross, which was to completely take the judgement for all men's sins on Himself.
I understand.
Through faith in Jesus, you'll also receive God's Spirit into your life. As we say 'yes' to His influence, we're changed to be more and more the people that we were created to become.
Really?
God wants to give you this green light! May I help you talk to Him right now?
Yes please.

Trucks
The load is what counts

(A truck is passing by)
Do you know that we are like trucks?
What do you mean?
We are filled with things. But if we are filled with wrong things, we can't enter Heaven.
Wrong things?
Impure thoughts, evil words, lies, hate, pride, greed, envy, selfishness, unforgiveness, indifference etc.
Hmm...
These things must be removed, they must be forgiven before we can enter Heaven. The good news is that someone is ready to forgive us, His name is Jesus.
I believe there is a God.
The important thing is to do what God wants. First of all He wants to forgive us and that is done when we turn away from sin and welcome Jesus into our lives.
I understand.
Do you want to have the wrong things in your life forgiven and removed by the only one who can do it?
Yes, I want that.
May I help you talk to God right now?
Please do.

Umbrella
Don't protect yourself from God

(It is raining)
You're protecting yourself from the rain.
Yes, I really don't like to be wet.
But I hope you don't protect yourself from the Gospel?
What do you mean?
Some people 'put up a cover' as soon as somebody begins to talk about God.
I understand, but I don't do that.
Great, to have an open heart toward God is a good beginning, next step is to do what God wants. Do you know what He wants?
Be nice to people, I suppose?
Yes, but we can't forget Him. He created us for fellowship with Himself and the Gospel is that Jesus came and died on the cross for the things we had done that separated God and us.
Hmm...
So what we need to do is to turn away from these things and believe that what He did on the cross was for us. Do you want to do that?
I think so.
God will not leave us alone without help in this world, but He wants to give us His own Spirit. God's Spirit on the inside of us will help us in all situations in life!
I think we need all help we can get. Do you want to begin this life today?
Absolutely.
May I help you talk to God right now?
Yes please.

Vacuum cleaner
Filled with dirt

(Your friend comes when you are vacuum cleaning)
Our lives are like a vacuum cleaner.
How do you mean?
As times goes by, we fill our lives with 'dirt'. Bad things, wrong things and unclean things.
Hmm...
The Word of God says; that before God will let us into Heaven, He will take a look on the inside of us.
(Open the vacuum cleaner and take out the trash bag). It will be a terrible day if we have to stand before Him with a bag full of unforgiven sins; lies, hate, pride, envy, selfishness, unforgivness, uncleanliness...
You're right...
The good news is that God did something so that we could get rid of the 'dirt'. He sent Jesus Christ to be crucified, so that we could stand clean and forgiven before our Creator!
That is good news indeed!
But we must do something; we must turn away from what the Word of God says is wrong and put our trust in Jesus. Are you ready to do that?
Absolutely.
May I help you talk to God right now?
Yes please.

Wages
The Wages of sin

Soon it is payday.
Yes, the best day of the month!
Haha, you're right.
Do you know that the Bible also talks about wages?
What kind of wages?
The wages of sin. The consequences of opening our hearts and lives for things not pleasing to God.
What are those consequences?
The Bible says: 'The wages of sin is death...' and here it means spiritual death, which is separation from God.
Sounds terrible.
Sin is terrible! But God is good and the rest of that verse says: 'the gift of God is eternal life in Christ Jesus.' When we turn away from sin, put our trust in Jesus and what He did for us on the cross, from that day we receive eternal life.
I understand.
May I help you talk to God right now?
Sure.

Wall
The most dangerous wall

(You are standing at a wall)
There are some good and some bad walls in the world.
What do you mean?
Good walls that guard and protect, but bad walls that separate and divide. Do you know the most dangerous wall?
No idea, please tell me.
The wall that we build between God and us.
What wall is that?
A wall of sin, a wall of things that are not pleasing to God. This wall separates Him and us.
I go to church sometimes.
That's a good beginning, but your wall will only come down when you make a decision in your heart, to turn away from what the Bible says is wrong and welcome Jesus into your life. He is the only one that can bring this wall down.
Hmm...
God wants your wall to come down today, so that you won't be separated anymore.
Okay.
May I help you talk to God right now?
Please.

Wallet
Better to lose

(Your friends wallet is on the table) Have you lost your wallet sometime?
One time, and it was not fun...
You're right, it's terrible to lose some things, but some things are wonderful to lose.
Like what?
The things in our lives that stop us from going to Heaven.
What do you mean?
The day when our lives here are over, everybody wants to go to Heaven, but if we are living in sin, Heaven will be closed for us.
What do you mean with sin?
Sin is disobedience to God, thoughts, words or actions. We need to lose these things if we want to enter into Heaven.
How can we do that?
Because of what Jesus did for us when he died on the cross. He took upon Himself all the sins of the world. We need to turn away from what we know are not pleasing to God, and put our trust in Jesus.
Okay.
That moment we 'lose' our sins and Heaven will be open for us.
Hmm...
Do you want to experience that?
Yes, I want that.
Are you open to do what is necessary?
I think so.
May I help you talk to God right now?
Please do.

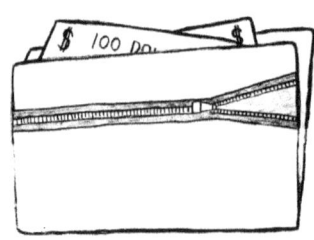

Wanted
You are wanted!

(In front of a 'wanted list')
It's interesting to see the 'wanted list'.
Yes, you're right.
Do you know that there also is a 'wanted list' in Heaven?
What do you mean?
God has a 'wanted list', and one of the people on that list is you!
Me?
Yes, God wants you, He wants you in His family. He wants you and
Him to have fellowship
Hmm...
So don't run away from Him anymore, run to Him. The way to God is open for us, because of what Jesus did on the cross. All the things we had done that had separated God and us, Jesus took upon Himself on the cross. When we put our trust in Him and in what He did for us, from that moment we are His!
I understand.
God wants you to come to Him today. He wants to give you His Spirit to help you know and do God's will. May I help you talk to Him right now?
Please do.

Wash
We must wash our hearts

(Somebody is washing up)
We wash many times during a lifetime.
Too many times…
But we can't forget to wash the most important thing.
What do you mean?
To wash our hearts, so that we can enter in to Heaven.
Please explain.
When life here is over, everybody wants to go to Heaven but because Heaven is a Holy place, no unforgiven sin can enter there, therefore we need to wash our hearts first.
How can we do that?
It was somebody that made it possible for us, His name is Jesus. He came to this world for a reason, it was to die on the cross and make it possible for man to be forgiven of their sins, and have their hearts washed.
Hmm…
What we need to do is to turn away from sin and welcome Jesus into our lives.
I understand.
Do you want your heart washed by the only one who can do it?
Yes.
When Jesus went to Heaven, He sent the Holy Spirit to us. The Holy Spirit is the one that will come and live on the inside of you, He will be your Helper.
Hmm…
May I help you talk to God right now?
Absolutely.

Weeds
The weeds in our hearts

(At a lawn)
Do you know that in a way, our hearts are like a lawn?
What do you mean?
The good things are the grass and the bad things are the weeds.
Great parable.
The problem is that the weeds in our hearts can't enter Heaven.
Hmm...
We need to call upon the one that can take away the weeds in our hearts. His name is Jesus, He can take them away because He died for them.
Can't I take them away myself?
No, no one can do that, we can't save ourselves, we need a Savior. The good news is that He is ready to take away the weeds in our hearts. Do you know when that happens?
No, please tell me.
When we turn to God and welcome Jesus as Lord of our lives.
Hmm...
The same Holy Spirit that was in Jesus will come and live in you. He will help you to know God's perfect will for your life, and do it! Do you want to begin this life today?
Absolutely.
May I help you talk to God right now?
Please do.

Wine
A greater miracle

(Somebody has a wine bottle)
Did you know that the first miracle Jesus did was to change water to wine?
Was it?
Yes, at a wedding. They ran out of wine, He did this miracle, and the party could go on.
Cool.
Yes, it was a cool miracle, but there is a much more important miracle He wants to do!
What?
He wants to forgive us our sins, so that we can go to Heaven.
So why doesn't He do that?
His forgiveness is available to everybody, but we must do something, we must act upon our own free will and ask Him for forgiveness.
Hmm...
The day we turn from sin to God and welcome Jesus into our lives, from that day we are forgiven, we belong to God, and we are on the way to Heaven.
I understand.
Do you want to experience that?
Yes.
May I help you talk to God right now?
Sure.

Word
The most important word

Do you know the most important word ever spoken?
No idea.
The word 'crucify', cried out by the people who wanted to kill Jesus.
Why was that so important?
If they hadn't called for His death, we could still be in our sins and the new covenant would not have been ratified by His blood.
I don't know if I have sinned.
You can have good intentions, but without God's Spirit helping you, the Bible makes clear that all men have sinned and fall short of the glory of God. Without God's help, it's impossible to live a life without sin and no sin can enter Heaven unforgiven.
Hmm...
We need the Savior, the one who died for our sins, rose again, and who today is ready to forgive us - His name is Jesus.
So what shall I do?
The good news is that the way is open to God. The Bible says that the moment you turn from sin and welcome Him in, you belong to God and are on your way to Heaven.
I see.
Is there anything that hinders you from coming to God right now?
I don't think so.
May I help you talk to Him now?
Please do.

World Trade Center
The designated pilot

(Somebody mentions 9/11)
9/11 is an interesting picture of many peoples' lives.
What do you mean?
Planes without their designated pilot, can cause a catastrophe.
Designated pilot?
There is only one correct pilot to take us to Heaven and His name is Jesus.
I'm my own pilot.
The problem is that you are not allowed into Heaven's airspace without permission. The things you've done that are not pleasing to God hinder you. Impure thoughts, evil words, lies, hate, pride, greed, envy, selfishness, unforgiveness, etc.
Hmm...
But because He died on the cross for these things and rose again as the Savior of the world, He is allowed to take those people to Heaven who choose Him as their "designated pilot" and Lord.
I understand.
Do you want Jesus to become your pilot to Heaven, your Savior?
I really want that.
May I help you talk to God right now?
Absolutely.

X-ray
God will x-ray us

I am getting an x-ray on my knee next week.
X-rays are interesting. It is great that doctors can see inside the body to help us, but do you know that one day God will x-ray us all?

What do you mean?
Before anyone can come into Heaven, God will x-ray our hearts to see if they are clean and ready for Heaven.

I think my heart is clean...
God's x-ray will show everything; the words we have spoken, what our eyes have looked upon, if we have opened our hearts for hate, pride, greed, selfishness, unforgiveness, jealousy etc.

Hmm...
Dirty hearts can't enter into Heaven. But God has the solution!

What is it?
He sent His Son to die on the cross for everyhting that made us dirty and guilty before Him. He did His part, our part is to turn away from sin and turn to Jesus. With Him in our lives we have forgiveness and nothing will stop us from going to Heaven.

It sounds great!
Heaven is the ultimate goal, but already now God wants fellowship with us and that we fulfill the destiny He has for each one of us.

I understand.
May I help you talk to God right now?

Please.

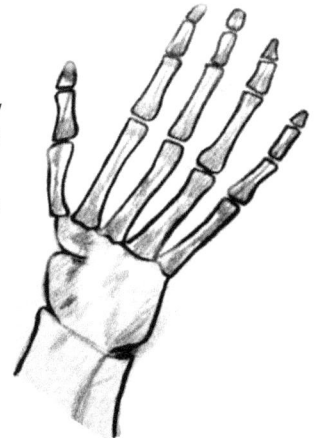

Praying *for* People

One of the most wonderful things that can happen to any of us is to come into contact with God, especially for the first time.

When we begin to speak with people about Jesus, repentance, forgiveness, healing and deliverance, they'll often begin to sense His presence. That's not strange, considering that the Holy Spirit has been actively waiting their whole life to convict them of sins and convince them about righteousness and judgement.

When we offer to pray for them, the sense of His presence will increase for many people, especially if their heart is open to the message we have just shared with them.

Please pray for them just as God leads you. However, if it's helpful, here's a suggestion of something that you can say to God and then pray for them as well:

"Father, thank you so much for sending Jesus into our world; that he lived a perfect life of love and was willing to die on the cross. Thank you that you've forgiven my sins, cleansed my heart and set me free from guilt, shame and bitterness.

Thank you for giving me your Holy Spirit, receiving me into your family and making me your child. Now I pray for 'Mark' that he will know the truth: that you love him and that Jesus died on the cross for him/her as well.

Please bless 'Mark' with faith and courage to open his heart and mind to you right now; that he could also receive your forgiveness and freedom, begin to know You and Your love, receive your Spirit and become your child for eternity. I ask all of this, in Jesus' name. Amen."

Praying *with* People

Something extraordinary happens when a person humbles himself before God, believes in Jesus' sacrifice on the cross, and invites Him to become Lord of their lives. God pays attention from heaven. Myriads of angels rejoice and the divine seed, the Holy Spirit, actually unites with their spirit. As they repent of their sins and walk in the light, they'll immediately have real and transparent fellowship with other disciples, and the blood of Jesus cleanses them from all sin: their own as well as the sins others have committed against them. What a blessing to leave behind our old life in baptism as well.

Jesus made it clear that some seed falls on hard ground, some by the wayside, some in the weeds and some into good ground. Our job is to sow and water; God will bring the increase. Angels will sort the wheat from the tares upon Jesus' return. Our job is to sow the seed, preach the gospel, share our testimony and to make disciples.

Some people are so prepared by God to give their lives to Him, that you can pray directly with them to do so. Others may become ready, especially after you pray *for* them. Here's a suggestion for praying with people, if they would like you to lead them in a prayer of salvation, where they repeat after you:

"Thank you God for sending Jesus to die on the cross, taking on Himself all my sins and forgiving me and cleansing me now, setting me free from all my guilt, pain, shame and bitterness.

Please give me your Holy Spirit and make me your son for eternity. Please renew my thought-life and transform me to be more and more like Jesus. I want to become the man that you created me to be. I trust you with all I am and have, and believe that you know what's best for my life in every area. Please be my Lord, now and forever. I ask all of this from you God, in Jesus' name. Amen."

Recommended books:

Become a Better You
by Joel Osteen

Before God's wrath
by H.L Nigro

Faith that Overcomes the World
by Ulf Ekman

Fourth Dimension
by Yonngi Cho

Goals
by Brian Tracy

God´s Blueprint for a Happy Home
by Lester Sumrall

How You Can be Led by the Spirit of God
by Kenneth Hagin

Is That Really You God?
by Loren Cunningham

One Thing You Can´t Do in Heaven
by Mark Cahill

Pilgrims' Progress
by John Bunyan

Purpose Driven Life
by Rick Warren

See You at the Top
by Zig Ziglar

Speak to Win
by Brian Tracy

Understanding the Purpose and Power of Prayer
by Myles Munroe

Your Best Life Now
by Joel Osteen

Recommended websites:

www.wayofthemaster.com
Excellent website for soulwinners

www.ontheredbox.com
Effective open-air evangelism in Europe

www.joelosteen.com
Pastor of the largest church in USA

www.briantracy.com
Life coach

Help us become better

We are grateful for all tips and feedback that you are willing to share. What was good? What was bad? What needs to be changed? Perhaps you have ideas for more 'conversation starters.' These will all help to make the next edition become a greater blessing. Thank you!

Please write to: info@21centurybooks.com or

International Arts & Media
Hagbergsgatan 31
415 06 Gothenburg, Sweden

www.ingramcontent.com/pod-product-compliance
Lightning Source LLC
LaVergne TN
LVHW021359080426
835508LV00020B/2360